LEVEL
2
SCIENCE
LET'S READ
AND
FIND OUT

DOWN COMES THE RAIN

BY FRANKLYN M. BRANLEY

ILLUSTRATED BY MARY ANN FRASER

HARPER

An Imprint of HarperCollinsPublishers

Special thanks to Don W. Hen and Dr. Sonia M. Kreidenweis,
professor of atmospheric science at Colorado State University,
for their expert advice.

The Let's-Read-and-Find-Out Science book series was originated by Dr. Franklyn M. Branley, Astronomer Emeritus and former Chairman of the American Museum of Natural History–Hayden Planetarium, and was formerly co-edited by him and Dr. Roma Gans, Professor Emeritus of Childhood Education, Teachers College, Columbia University. Text and illustrations for each of the books in the series are checked for accuracy by an expert in the relevant field. For more information about Let's-Read-and-Find-Out Science books, write to HarperCollins Children's Books, 195 Broadway, New York, NY 10007, or visit our website at www.letsreadandfindout.com.

Let's Read-and-Find-Out Science® is a trademark of HarperCollins Publishers.

HarperCollins
PUBLISHERS
· Since 1817 ·

ISBN 978-0-06-238664-9 (trade bdg.) — ISBN 978-0-06-238663-2 (pbk.)

The artist used acrylic and colored pencil on paper to create the illustrations for this book.
Typography by Erica De Chavez. 16 17 18 19 20 SCP 10 9 8 7 6 5 4 3 2 1 ❖ Revised edition, 2017

To Abigail Samoun
—M. A. F.

Rain comes from clouds.
It comes from big clouds and little clouds.
It comes from black clouds, white clouds, and gray clouds.

All clouds—big ones and little ones, gray ones and white ones—are made of billions of tiny drops of water. The drops are called **droplets**, because they are so small.

If this is the size of a drop of water, a droplet would be just a tiny speck, even smaller than this one.

Drop   Droplet

Water droplets come from **water vapor.** Water vapor is a gas.

There's always water vapor in the air, but you can't SEE it . . .

. . . can't SMELL it . . .

. . . and you can't FEEL it.

Water vapor is made when water **evaporates**.
That means the water changes from a liquid to a gas.

In the morning, put a teaspoon of water in a saucer. By that night, it may have evaporated into the air!

When wet clothes hang on the clothesline, the water in them evaporates. The heat from the sun changes the water drops and droplets into water vapor.

Just like the heat from the stove changes water in the kettle to water vapor. If you heat it long enough, all the water boils away. The water vapor goes into the air.

13

Most of the water vapor in the air comes from lakes, rivers, and oceans. It comes from the leaves of plants and from the wet ground.

14

Heat from the sun causes the water to evaporate. The water changes from a liquid to a gas and the water vapor goes into the air.

15

When you breathe out, you put water vapor into the air. Usually, you cannot see the water vapor. But it is there.

Sometimes, if it's cold, you can see your breath. That's because the water vapor **condenses**. It changes from a gas to a little cloud.

When cows, horses, dogs, and cats breathe out, they put water vapor into the air, too. On a cold day, the water vapor changes to droplets and makes little clouds you can see.

You can make water vapor change to water. Put a lot of ice into a glass of water.

As the glass gets *colder*, the outside of the glass gets WET.

Water vapor in the air is condensing on the glass.

There may be so much condensation that the glass drips.

Sometimes the glass stays dry. That means there is not much water vapor in the air.

The air holds the water vapor. Breezes carry it from one place to another.

Much of the vapor moves up and away from the earth.

Water droplets growing by combining with each other to form larger drops

Water vapor condensing to form droplets

Rising water vapor

* This is not visible to the human eye.

Air above the earth is *always* cold. The higher you go, the colder it gets. When air gets cold enough, the water vapor in it condenses. The vapor changes to water droplets. The water droplets make clouds.

When clouds are thick and dark,
they are holding much more water.

When clouds are thin and wispy,
they are holding only a little water.

A single droplet is so small you cannot see it. But you can see a cloud. That's because there are millions and millions and millions of water droplets in a cloud.

Inside the clouds, droplets join together to make drops. When the drops are too heavy to stay up in the clouds, they fall to earth.

The sky is full of them. They fall through the air and splatter on the ground. They are raindrops.

Sometimes there are only a few small raindrops that fall slowly. It is drizzling.

Sometimes there are lots of big drops that fall very fast. Now it is pouring.

Sometimes the drops in clouds **freeze**. These raindrops become ice crystals. This can happen even on a hot summer day.

Some clouds may be higher than most airplanes ever go. The higher the clouds, the colder they are. That's because the clouds and water droplets are high above the earth. Many clouds are so high that they are freezing cold.

In these high, cold clouds, water vapor changes to droplets, and the droplets change to drops. The drops freeze into ice.

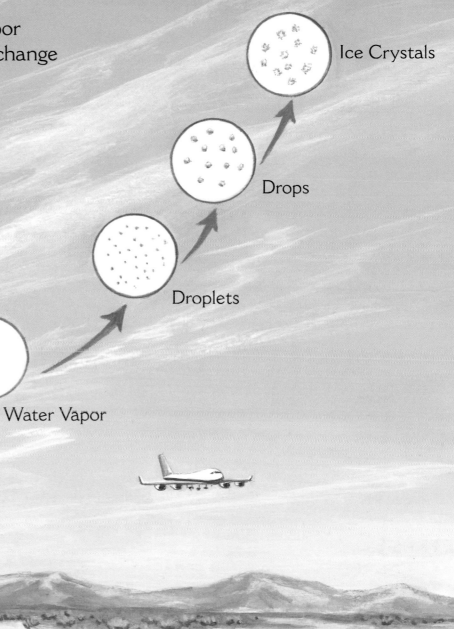

Ice Crystals

Drops

Droplets

Water Vapor

Inside the cloud, these tiny bits of ice start to fall, but they don't *always* fall out of the cloud. Instead, they may be carried *upward* by air that is moving away from the earth.

As they are carried upward, more water collects on the tiny bits of ice. When that water freezes, the crystals of ice have another layer on them.

The ice crystals are now heavier, so once more they fall toward the earth. But air moving away from the earth may carry the ice crystals upward again. Higher and higher they go, and another layer of ice freezes onto them.

The ice crystals get heavier and heavier. They get so heavy that the air can no longer carry them upward.

So the ice crystals fall to the earth. It is raining ice.

The ice crystals grow larger and fall to the earth as **hailstones**. They may be the size of your fingernail or they may be as big as golf balls, or even bigger.

In 1970, hailstones as big as *softballs* fell on Kansas. Fields of corn were FLATTENED by the hailstones!

Hailstones are not *stones*. They're pieces of ICE. So
when it hails, go inside so you're not hit on the head!
When it stops hailing, go outside and pick up a hailstone.
Break it in two, and you will see the layers of ice.

Hailstone Ice Layers

Water in the clouds can make HAIL.

Water in the clouds makes RAIN too.

When it stops raining or hailing, the sun comes out.
Once more, water evaporates.

Water evaporates from lakes, rivers, and oceans.

It evaporates from the leaves of plants and from the wet ground.

The water changes to water vapor.
It's carried up and away from the earth,
where the air is cool, or even freezing.

34

When the water vapor cools, it condenses. The water vapor changes to water droplets, and all together the droplets make clouds.

Water droplets join together to make water drops. The drops fall to the earth from the clouds.

Once more it is raining.

GLOSSARY

Condense: Change from a gas to a liquid.

Droplet: A tiny drop of water.

Evaporate: Change from a liquid to a gas.

Freeze: Change from a liquid to a solid.

Hailstone: Heavy ice that falls from a cloud.

Water vapor: Water as a gas.

FIND OUT MORE ABOUT RAIN
Cycle in a Baggie

What do each of the steps of the water cycle look like? To find out, you will need a plastic bag with a resealable top, a permanent marker, water, tape, and a window that gets direct sunlight.

Using your permanent marker, draw a water cycle on your baggie, being sure to mark condensation, evaporation, and precipitation.

Put ¼ cup of water in the bottom of the bag, close it up, and tape it to the window. For the next few days, observe your baggie: Is it clear? Are the sides foggy, or do they have water drops?

The water in the bag is getting heated by the sun and evaporating. The gas then tries to escape from the bag, but when it touches the sides, it cools down and condenses again, dripping back down into the baggie.

This book meets the Common Core State Standards for Science and Technical subjects. For Common Core resources for this title and others, please visit www.readcommoncore.com.

Be sure to look for all of these books in the Let's Read-and-Find-Out Science series: